MW00931782

Healing with Quantum Energy

Ryu Takahashi

ISBN: 9-783-8391-4363-6

Published by:

Books on Demand GmbH - Norderstedt, Germany

The law of attraction

FOREWORD

Every person notices quantum energy
– every day

This book is written for those who know that reality contains more than that described in orthodox psychology and physics. Those who know that there are things that exist for which there is perhaps no explanation, but which nevertheless work. This book is also written for those who prefer to be convinced of the truth through experience instead of loosing themselves in the endless theorizing of scientific theses.

Yet this book is also directed at all doubters, whom I should like to invite simply to leave their doubts in the cloakroom and engage with the insights of hands-on experience. Is it not just possible that there is something to be found in this 'energy thing?' Perhaps it is actually possible to use energy to trigger healing.

I say "**YES – IT IS POSSIBLE**." Moreover, I say it as someone who had ignored, indeed vilified spirituality and esotericism his whole life; someone, who had always believed in and lived strictly and exclusively according to the doctrines of orthodox science. Even now, I am not a convinced esoteric. However, I owe my ability to say unhesitatingly, "YES – IT IS POSSIBLE" not to any theory or story, but my hands-on experience. Moreover, I should like to invite you to make this very same experience. Right now.

ENERGY IS NOT A SECRET

All-embracing energy is truly no secret. There are a great number of people working with quantum energy. Some call it Reiki, others Ki or Chi, but they all mean one and the same thing. Indeed, the number of people who believe in the efficacy of quantum energy and use it is greater than the number of doubters who deny its existence. The number of people using quantum energy alone in Asia is greater as the population of many other countries.

Unfortunately, this new thought, with its expanded consciousness is being taken up only slowly in our civilization. Why so? On the one hand, we have a very powerful pharmaceutical lobby hostile to any effective method of self-help. On the other hand, there are those who just do not want to learn new techniques. These people start with scientific explanations and finish in helplessness. In effect, they live according to the maxim: what science cannot explain does not exist. Fortunately; you the reader, do not number amongst such people, otherwise you would not be reading this book. You are open to new experiences and prepared to embark on new journeys into an expanded consciousness. That makes me very happy.

Realistic people are should be prepared to concede that there are simply a number of things that work for which we do not have an explanation. Prepare yourself to work with quantum energy without taking it too seriously. Try some of the exercises without putting yourself under any pressure. You do not have to succeed at the first attempt. Nothing is less helpful than doggedness and pressure. You have nothing to loose - or do you? Let yourself be surprised just how easy it is.

> Many people already work with energy.
>
> Do not take the matter too seriously.
>
> Try it out without any pressure.

CONSCIOUSNESS AND THE MIND

When we speak of consciousness, then we usually mean our mind. Nevertheless, this entirely wrong. Our mind is often exactly the very instance that serves to block our consciousness. As this could sound rather confusing, I should like to explain it as well as I can. Consciousness is a state of absolute awareness of the moment. Without thoughts, without an appreciation of time, simply BEING. The full and exclusive concentration on a single point, on one thing and only this thing - this is consciousness. Consciousness does not exist in the past or the future. It has existence only in the immediate here and now. How often do we indulge ourselves in a past which we are no longer able to influence? How often do we worry about the future – this has nothing to do with the consciousness. Thus is the influence of our thoughts; our mind drives us to engage with these things. In one sense, our mind is a blessing as it prevents us from repeating the same mistakes over and over. It allows us to plan our future and warns us of impending danger. Nevertheless, if unable to control it, our mind holds us from enjoying consciousness, it can become a curse. It blocks the most important precondition for the use of quantum energy - the moment of consciousness. Nevertheless, all is not lost. We can learn to control our mind more easily than we think. Engage with the exercises described in this book - you might just be surprised.

Attempt the following exercise. It really does not require great effort.

- Find a place where you are undisturbed.

- Sit down, close your eyes and just sit and observe your thoughts. Without becoming active - simply allow the thoughts to come and go.

- After having done that for a little while, ask yourself the question "why am I thinking right now?" This is usually followed by a pause, a period of absolute calm in your head.

Exactly this pause, this calm is absolute consciousness.

Initially, the pause lasts just for a short while, but upon repetition of the exercise it becomes longer. You can vary the question for example "where is my consciousness located?" or "how large is my consciousness?" Just enjoy the absolute calm in your head whilst your mind is distracted, trying to find an answer to your (rather difficult) question.

You have made the first important experiences in the successful use of quantum energy. It is this simple, even if you find it difficult to believe. Just wait and see.

Understanding blocks your consciousness
Consciousness exists only here and now
Consciousness is the absence of thoughts –
absolute calm

THE VARIOUS HEALING SYSTEMS
AVAILABLE ON THE MARKET

Sooner or later, all those working with healing and even those who have discovered a 'gift' for healing others which they hold as being exceptional, will discover various different systems of healing. Despite all the different names and applications, they all have on thing in common: every system claims to be the only, the best, energy-richest or even most holy. They all have a list of rules as long as your arm which it is necessary to observe, symbols to use, and sometimes even angels and spirits to conjure up. They warn against negative energies which can be abused by beings from other dimensions to damage the user. Often, the patient has to part with horrendously large sums of money to be initiated in Reiki or similar systems, so that you too can receive the 'gift' of healing. The initiations contain many steps, and you are not always ready for the next higher step. There are even long-distance initiations to be bid for at auctions.

As you can see, the healing industry has spawned an enormous market, generating an annual turnover of millions. This is all extreme nonsense, then you do not need a special initiation, or the permission of any particular celestial being (although you are free to believe in what you please) for one person to initiate the healing of another. You do not need any symbols to activate allegedly different energies in order to enable someone to synchronize their oscillations. None of this is necessary, as everybody possesses the 'gift' of healing, or of synchronizing other people. You just need to allow it to happen without engaging in any theories. Give the exercises in this book a chance and engage with the feelings that you experience. Forget any sort of initiation, angels or miraculous loss of money.

> Everyone has access to energy.
>
> Initiation is not necessary.
>
> There is no such thing as negative energy - energy is always neutral.

THE EFFECT OF OUR THOUGHTS

Having expressed a limited hostility to theories, I do not want to deprive my more theory-interested readers from their satisfaction. Simply put, I shall explain a few basic facts about quantum physics without going into overmuch detail. If you are interested in finding out more about the subject, the book market is awash with titles from authors who know a lot more about the subject than I. Indeed, an awareness of the various theories relating to quantum energy is not necessary for understanding its significance. Nevertheless, such knowledge does help those people who need an explanation for what they do. It is necessary to bear in mind that although many have posed the question as to how the world actually works, this question cannot be answered with complete security.

Let us investigate the control of our perception. A significant factor in this process is our expectation. Indeed, our various expectations play an important role in deciding how we conceive of and understand the world around us. In doing so, the word perception describes an <u>active</u> process – we perceive something. Let us use an example: earlier scholars thought that the world was flat and that the over-inquisitive traveller would fall off the other side should he reach the extent of the earth. They perceived the world as being flat. Only experience taught us that it was possible to sail around the world without falling off. This experience created a new truth. The earth is round. Exactly the same applies to healing with quantum energy. If we reject the existence of quantum energy out of hand then we shall never be able to use it. If on the other hand, we make the experience that this energy both exists and is accessible to all, it is easy to use it and achieve the corresponding 'miracles.' The only precondition is that we let it happen. Indeed, this represents everything other than a 'miracle,' then everybody can do it. Quantum energy is available to humankind, and always has been. Unfortunately, our distorted perception often makes us feel helpless in the face of circumstances. We find all nature of scapegoats for our situation except from ourselves and our own actions. We conceive of ourselves as entirely isolated from all external influences, other people and the rest of the world.

Fortunately, there are a number of other ways of seeing the world and ourselves, developed using new insights from quantum physics. The picture of the world painted by these findings enables us to cast off old patterns of faith which have proven themselves to be of little use, and to replace them with a new, more positive, energy-rich consciousness. Unfortunately however, humankind is slow to take up these insights and the new perspectives which they offer, if indeed, they are accepted at all. It is very difficult to cast off old, accepted attitudes. People are creatures of habit, as tried and trusted patterns of living and behaviour bring a sense of security. As a result, we are often resistant to new insights which threaten to alter our view of the world. I should like to encourage you to examine your own form of perception. Perhaps it would be helpful for you to experience things which you previously held to be unthinkable. Perhaps this book will lead you to experience something causing a fundamental shift in your view of the world. One thing is clear: without trying it, you will never find out whether it is true.

For all those seeking an explanation of the existence of quantum energy, I will now examine the topic a little more closely. Initially, quantum physics provides only theories requiring verification. Proving these theories is only possible through trial and error, i.e. experience. What use are the best measurement instruments when it later becomes clear that all they have done is to quantify an illusion?

In order to establish the effect of thought on the outside world, you should first pose the question as to the nature of the world and all real things. We have to ask the question: what exactly is matter? The majority of people would tell you "matter is solid and consists of atoms."

Yet this is only half of the matter. Let us investigate the question in more detail. Atoms have a core circuited by electrons. The atom core consists of neutrons and protons, themselves consisting of quarks. Science assumes that the quarks are formed from prequarks. Thus in one sense, we could feel justified in claiming that matter is something solid.

Yet the question is: what is to be found between the atom and the atom core? The answer: emptiness, indeed, an emptiness which makes up the majority of the whole. Matter consists predominantly of empty space. The deeper we probe into matter, the more of a vacuum we find. Yet why do we perceive solid objects? This is the part taken by quantum energy. The void interacts with the matter to create a huge energy field. This is why objects appear as we see them.

If we believe this version of events, then the void, the emptiness, is a real existing physical substance pervading the whole universe. Quantum energy thus pervades everything that we see. It penetrates all objects and all organisms. If this quantum energy connects everything, then we should also be able to utilize this energy. We can use it to influence objects and people and we can use it to initiate healing. Then thoughts are also material, and are connected with the void and thus the quantum energy. What else should it exist of? In essence, everything is quantum energy – feelings, thoughts, matter. What is more, you can make use of it.

Expectation creates reality – we often perceive
what we expect.
What we believe influences our perception.
A void is a physical substance – energy.
Everything in the universe is pervaded by the
physical substance, this void.

OUR OWN SYNCHRONIZATION

Before beginning this chapter I should like to
repeat that the healing processes described in
this book only makes sense to me when presented in the following fashion. I have based
my descriptions on the insights and theories of
quantum physics. This does not mean that they
function exactly in this manner, but one thing is
sure - they actually work. Surely, the how and
the why of the world is of only secondary im-

portance when we find ourselves in a position to help people?

It is important that you realise something very important. We are unable to heal directly, but are in the position to initiate the healing process in our patients. Your patient reacts to the impulses which you transfer to him: the actual healing itself is effected by quantum energy, not you the healer. Illness is usually the result of an unsynchronized system, the oscillations of which now run in diametrical opposition. If you succeed in re-synchronizing the system on the elementary level, you can succeed in stimulating the healing process over the long-term.

To re-synchronize the system of another person, and thus heal him, it is necessary that your own oscillations are entirely synchronized during treatment. This means that you need first to have brought your own oscillations to a unitary, relaxed level before beginning with the treatment itself. Should your own oscillations be asynchronous, even chaotic, you will transfer this state to your patient and exercise a detrimental effect on the healing process.

In order to be able to initiate a successful healing process, you first need to learn to synchronize yourself. A pleasant method of doing this is described in the following passages. It represents only one method amongst many, but should you use it, you will sense how your personal energy levels increase after regular use. Synchronous oscillations release energy - chaotic oscillations block energy. Try it and you will see what I mean.

Exercise (lasts approx. 5-10 minutes)

- Sitting on a chair, loosen all your muscles entirely.

- Place your hands on your thighs; clasp them slightly into a fist.

- Concentrate exclusively on the sensation in your right hand for about 1 minute.

- Shift your attention to your left foot. Concentrate exclusively on the sensation in your left foot - notice the difference between it and your right hand (also for approx. 1 minute).

- Breathe deeply in and out a few times. Allow your breathing to become deeper and more relaxed.

- Concentrate on both your right hand and left foot simultaneously. Think five times "my hand and foot are absolutely identical."

- Feel how the sensation in both limbs is identical.

You do not need to follow this procedure exactly; perhaps you prefer to use other body parts. This is no problem. You will notice how strongly our psyche can affect our body. What is more, it does not just affect your body, but also your environment. Then as popular wisdom would have it, 'the inside is reflected on the outside.' The psyche is an important point when seeking to initiate healing with quantum energy. We will learn more about this later. Take a little time after every exercise to return from your relaxed position. Becoming active too soon could have disagreeable consequences such as dizziness or headache.

Healing is automatic; we merely activate it.
Illness is the result of opposing oscillations.
Synchronization produces oscillatory parity.
The healer must oscillate synchronously during treatment.

> Synchronous oscillations releases energy; chaotic oscillations block energy.

EXERCISES TO PRODUCE SYNCHRONY

Here are two further exercises to keep you from boredom, favourable to synchronization. You can combine them with the previous exercise or alternate them. If you do not like the exercises, simply make up your own. It is not important to keep to any specific rules or specifications. It is important that you feel comfortable during the exercises and that you see what has changed and believe that your own methods actually works. Play a little music, or just establish absolute silence - just as YOU like. You are familiar with the principle.

29

Remember what I told you: don't take the
whole thing too seriously!

If you do this, I can guarantee that it works.

Please note: ensure that you conduct the exercises whilst sitting down. This improves your
concentration. Lying down allows your attention to wander and you could start dreaming or
even fall asleep.

Exercise 1:

- Sitting on a chair, loosen all your muscles entirely.
- Place your hands on your thighs
- Breathe in and out deeply (10 times).
  Increase the interval between breaths
  very slowly. Ensure that the pauses do
  not become too long, and that you get
  enough air.

- With every breath, imagine a spiral of light shining onto your body. The spiral becomes ever-larger until it envelops your whole body.

- Imagine that the spiral brings your whole body into harmony. All your oscillations are influenced by the spiral and run in a single direction.

- A pleasant feeling begins to establish itself. Observe how this feeling extends across your whole body. Once you notice that this sensation has synchronized your entire body, the exercise is completed.

Exercise 2:

For this exercise you need that talent for visualization, which can of course, be learnt.

- Assume the same position as in exercise 1
- Imagine that your thoughts are revolving in a spiral. All words and pictures are moving in an upwards-revolving spiral.
- Now imagine that this upwards-revolving spiral is slowing down. It is moving ever-more slowly like a tornado loosing speed. It becomes slower and slower until it starts to disintegrate.
- As soon as the thought spiral has disintegrated, you will notice a moment of absolute consciousness, a thought vacuum. Attempt to maintain this vacuum as long as possible.

- End the exercise as soon as the first thoughts return.

You will notice that the thought vacuum, the period of absolute consciousness, becomes longer with practice.

Try to incorporate these synchronization exercises into your everyday life. They provide the foundation for successful healing.

We all know people who seem to rob us of our energy. We begin to feel bad the moment they enter the room. Their negative charisma is so overwhelming that we crave to leave the room immediately. These people are asynchronous. Their problems, their negative thoughts and imbalance disturb any kind of harmony. Such people are unable to initiate a natural, equalized oscillation in others. On the contrary, they introduce chaos into the ordered systems of those around them. You should attempt, wherever possible, to ensure that such chaos does not obtain the upper hand in you. Synchronize yourself as often as is possible. You will be amazed how quickly a positive effect is able to unfold in your self and your life in general.

Do not take the matter too seriously!

Synchronize yourself regularly.

Practice makes perfect.

(progress sets in fast)

THE MENTAL LEVEL

No doubt you are asking yourself if it is really so easy. Can I really equalize my oscillation patterns myself? Just by thinking about it? Indeed, without an awareness of the power of the mental level over our bodies, it is a very difficult proposition to believe. Nevertheless, it is easy. Our bodies always react to our thoughts, whether conscious or unconscious. Indeed, this reaction is not just restricted to our bodies. Our immediate surroundings and other people also react to our thoughts. Thoughts exist - this is not contested by anyone - and our thoughts are noticed by others. Cast your mind back to the last time that you looked at someone that you loved and immediately knew what they were thinking. Or what you felt as someone close to you was suffering without you having first seen them. Nevertheless, you knew that something was wrong. These examples show that it is extremely important that we employ our thoughts consciously and that we expunge everything from ourselves which could damage those around us. Thought hygiene brings considerable advantages and strengthens our healing effect on other people.

For example, I have given up watching the news and reading a newspaper; then it is far from conducive to spreading peace and happiness. The news consists almost exclusively of war, hate, deceit, unhappiness and murder. Such factors serve to makes us afraid. Fear produces oscillations similar to a hurricane. In doing so, we block the mechanisms of self-healing and are unable to help others. When was the last time that you heard of news item reporting happiness, prosperity and joy? I rest my case. Journalists want to spread fear as the fearful are easier to control. Fear makes timid and timidity prevents independent thought. This is why I avoid negative input of all nature. In doing so, I feel much better. Try it yourself for a week.

Allow yourself a measure of pleasure every day. When getting up, avoid thinking about the unpleasant tasks lying ahead of you. Simply remind yourself of the last happy experience that you had, for example, the last loving words from your partner. Focus on the good things in your life. I concede, it is not easy, and requires a certain discipline and strength, but it is very much worth it. Your life will change fundamentally when you shift your focus from problems to the pleasant things in life. In doing so, you will notice these nice things more often in every day life. You will start the day in a balanced fashion, and your oscillations will change. It will not take long until the people in your life seek your company and try to take advantage of your healing powers.

You will be surprised every day at the small

miracles occurring around you and at the small

miracles which you work yourself.

Negative information generates chaos.

Allow yourself daily pleasure.

INCREASING YOUR SENSITIVITY

Some people are 'energy-sensitive' by nature; they have the ability to perceive the energy of others. The distance over which they can do this depends on their receptiveness. This is nothing unusual or supernatural; we all possess this ability. Unfortunately however, this is gift has atrophied in many people. This could be a result of media saturation or the ever-greater passivity with which we shape our spare time. We have become obsessed with the images presented to us and rely on our ears and eyes at the expense of our intuition or instinct. Neglecting these powers means that sooner or later we become entirely impervious to their very existence. What is more, we become ever-more unfeeling. The good news is that we can train our intuition and sensitivity. It is not lost, it merely needs reactivation. All you need is practice. I should like to describe an exercise which helps to perceive energy consciously.

- Sit on a chair and close your eyes
- With your hands at shoulder position, lead them together until the palms of your hands are touching each other.
- Concentrate on the palms of your hands. Observe when they perceive your aura. Our aura, our energy field, can manifest itself through heat or a certain prickling.

- As soon as they perceive the aura, form an imaginary energy ball in your hands. Play with your perception.

Initially, the majority of people perceive their aura only after their hands touch. Repetition of this exercise increases the distance at which you can perceive your aura. You can also conduct this exercise with a partner. Sit opposite your partner and close your eyes. Then, move your hands slowly towards his body until you perceive his aura. You will notice that you can perceive those with a lot of energy at their disposal from a far greater distance.

Daily repetition of this exercise will enable you to increase your power of perception extremely rapidly. You do not even require a great deal of time, and you can practice anywhere. After you have got used to the exercise, pay great attention to the feeling in your hands when a person enters the room. Often, you can notice that the palms of your hands begin to prickle. This happens with people who need energy and who draw it towards them unconsciously. They are using you as a channel.

We can feel energy.

Perception increases with

exercise - practice daily.

PREPARING A SESSION

Unlike many systems of healing, preparation for a session does not involve the fixation on techniques and methods. In essence, you are preparing yourself to do nothing. You are getting ready to achieve absolutely synchronous oscillation for the session; perfect balance and harmony.

Is that all? Yes, that is all.

No further preparation is necessary. Your oscillations will enable you to transfer the power of your mental level to your patient. It ensures that the healing process is initiated without requiring any great effort.

When approached by a person, you feel his presence at a particular distance. You also often feel that a person is full of power and positive energy. That proves that you also have an effect on other people. The only difference is that you will now do it consciously. You know that your state, your frequency of oscillation is transferrable to other people. That is all that you need to know. You do not need anything else to be able to heal someone.

42

You will probably develop your own ritual of preparation over time. Whilst not strictly necessary, it can prove to be a great help in adapting to the person whom you wish to help. Indeed, with practice, you will require ever-less time for an impending session. The tighter a grasp you have on your mental level, the longer you will be able to fixate on your absolute consciousness (the mental void), and the easier it will be to find it.

Prepare to do nothing!
Your oscillations transfer themselves.
Use ritual where it helps.

THE COURSE OF THE SESSION

The session should be conducted in a calm, relaxed atmosphere in which both you and the patient feels comfortable and relaxed. Ensure that all disruptive influences are excluded. You, the healer, should be present in the here and now of your mental level. Do not bathe in the thoughts of the past or future. Let the patient explain their problem precisely. The patient says for example, "I have a pain in my right shoulder." Now formulate your aim in precise thoughts for example: "a normal, functioning shoulder free of any pain."

Now begin with one of the methods described in the following chapters, or construct a method yourself, which accords more closely to your own conceptions. You need not restrict your-selves around the methods presented here; rather you are absolutely free to develop your own method. In doing so, it is important that your mental level is in the correct state. That is the wonderful thing about quantum energy. It can be used anywhere and everywhere. No rules, symbols or initiation necessary.

Be present in the here and now – absolute consciousness!

Listen to the problem carefully.

Formulate your aim positively and precisely.

Start with your method.

VARIOUS METHODS

A session can be structured in a number of different ways. Now that you know that rule keeping is entirely unnecessary, you can apply the following models just as you like - either entirely faithfully, or adapted to any extent. The only thing of importance is that your oscillations are in perfect harmony.

For physical complaints

Ask your patient to indicate the location of their pain. Ask him to move the painful area so that you can assess the degree of restriction from which he suffers. Now place your hand on the area in question and apply light pressure. Be careful not to cause too much pain. If it is not possible to touch this area, just hold your hand a centimetre away from the location of the pain. Concentrate on this area for (3-5 minutes) paying attention to the feeling presented by the muscle and tissue. You will notice the development of amazing warmth in a short time.

Now place your hand on a healthy area. Concentrate on this area and how it feels.

Finally, concentrate on both hands and picture (precisely and positively) the desired state of health. Notice the change in feeling in both hands until both feel the same. Now end the session.

Mental complaints

Sit your patient on a chair, with his face to the chair back. Sitting behind him, ask him to close his eyes and breathe in and out ten times. Now place each hand on his left and right shoulder (it is better that he remove his upper clothing). In your mind, concentrate on the quantum energy flow from your hands into his body. Maintain this state for 3-5 minutes.

Place both hands underneath the patient's neck adjacent to the spine for a short time so that the spine is directly between your hands. Focus your thoughts on synchronizing the patient's oscillations. Imagine that your own inner harmony is flowing through your hands into the patient's spine and is then through his entire body. Maintain deep, calm breathing for a further 2-3 minutes. Now end the session.

You have probably noticed that the treatment described for both sessions never lasts for longer than 10 minutes. As the effects of treatment with quantum energy lasts several days, a longer session is usually unnecessary. Nevertheless, you should feel completely free to conduct the session for longer than the 10 minutes described here. Rely on your feelings and instinct. With increasing practice and conviction in your own skills, you will require considerably less time. Indeed, the healing process can be initiated in a matter of seconds.

At this point, before throwing the book away in disbelief, I should like to take the opportunity to remind you that the earth was still not flat even when the majority of society was convinced of the proposition. Give the book a try - let yourself be convinced.

> The length of the session depends
> on your instinct.
> The effects of quantum energy last
> several days after the session.

AFTER THE SESSION

Due to the state of deep relaxation brought about very shortly after the application of a quantum energy treatment it is necessary to grant the patient a few minutes to come round. Make sure to obtain feedback about his condition - how did he experience the treatment? What was he thinking during the session? Has his pain decreased or even disappeared?

Some people react very quickly to quantum energy. Others feel absolutely nothing during and after treatment. Often, the results of the treatment are recognized only in the days following the session. Ensure to arrange a follow-up consultation session about a week after the initial consultation. Prepare a questionnaire which you can use to evaluate the treatment. This provides valuable feedback with which to assess your success.

Quantum energy always produces harmony. It always leads to healing, even when it is not immediately noticeable. This is because the process of synchronization does not proceed identically in every person. You will also notice that after treatment, you always feel calm, balanced and peaceful. Quantum energy has just as curative an effect on the practitioner as the patient. That is the good thing about it. You can apply quantum energy as often as you wish - it is impossible to do any damage with it. There are no risks - there is no such thing as 'negative energy.' The application of quantum energy always results in order and harmony.

Give the patient time to 'come around.'
Quantum energy always produces harmony.
Use quantum energy as often as you
wish - there are no risks or side-effects.

You have already learnt how quantum energy can be used as an agent of self-help. Simply apply one of the methods which I have described to your self. That is it.

Now of course, you would require impressive acrobatic skills should you wish to place both your hands on your own shoulder blades. Remaining relaxed in this position is almost impossible. Nevertheless, instead of your shoulders, you can place your hands on your solar plexus, or on anywhere else that you can reach. It will work just as well. There are no rules, dogmas or anything else to follow or abide by. If you are feeling relaxed and comfortable, quantum energy will create harmony. It is really quite simple. If you want to activate your powers of self-healing and synchronize your oscillations then create a calm, relaxed atmosphere or just sit down and rely on your intuition. After a while, notice how your body begins to change during the self-treatment, and with it, your own perception of it. Try to establish a mental void and abandon yourself to absolute conscious-ness. Even if this does not always work straight away, the quantum energy will still work. You will feel this quite clearly.

> You can even use quantum energy successfully on yourself.
> Trust, do not be over-analytic

OPEN TO ALL

I would like to claim that everyone can use quantum energy to heal others. All those pre-pared to engage with this new experience can become a healer. My assurance in making this claim is located in my experience. I also numbered amongst those who rejected everything which could not be proven or explained scientifically. Despite my Asian roots I rejected everything smacking of Reiki, hypnotism or homeopathy as just a quack swindle designed to dupe the gullible. Nevertheless, one day I arrived at the point at which my physical and mental problems threatened to get the better of me and was unable to find help in the orthodox medical science. In my despair, I turned to therapists offering an 'alternative.' Initially, I was sceptical that hypnosis and positive energy could have any sort of effect, but seeing no other way out of my predicament, I gave it a chance. Today, I am grateful for the disorder which prevailed in me as it forced me to widen my horizons. I now know that things which science and medicine are unable to grasp are indeed possible. Perhaps they are not beyond belief; it is just that some people want to prevent us from knowing about them. It is worth consideration.

Overwhelmed by what I experienced with the new therapists, I began to investigate the subject of energy. Whilst studying the relevant material it became clear that a great number of people market an even greater number of systems all aiming at the same end: healing. Every system tries to establish itself as the best, with its own energy as the most powerful and effective. Despite my change in attitude, I still maintained a residual amount of healthy scepticism, and asked myself whether it is possible that various energies exist side by side. I studied a number of subjects, including quantum physics and began to experiment. I eventually reached the conclusion that every system describes the same thing. Just as the major religions all refer to the same God, so do all the various methods of healing refer to quantum energy. Every system uses the same source. Moreover, my experiments brought me to the conclusion that we do not need any particular system. Nor do we need any symbols or initiation in quantum energy. Quantum energy pervades everything in the universe. Quantum energy also pervades us: you me and our fellow human beings. Simply everything. Already in possession of the necessary skill, we do not need to receive anything, just to learn how to use them. What is more, it is extremely simple. Try it … everyone can do it!

Quantum physics provide plausible
explanations
but
Experience is a greater truth
than any scientific explanation.

JUST WHY IT IS SO SIMPLE

As you have no doubt noticed, I have said right from the beginning that the application of quantum energy is extremely easy. Simply trust me and then experience it by experimenting with the techniques that I have demonstrated. If you still do not believe me, then I should like to make one more attempt to convince you.

Are you the sort of person who 'only believes what he sees?' If so, I should like to ask you what gravity looks like. Gravity is not visible, but is exists. In the same manner, thoughts and feeling also exist without us being able to see them. You perceive them just in the same way as you perceive gravity. Why should you not be able to perceive the energy pervading your very body? Thoughts, feelings (love, hate etc.) consist of energy, and this energy can have very strong effects on us. You have no doubt experienced this yourself. You perceive far much more energy as you would like to believe. Previously, you have done this passively. Start to control energy using your thoughts and feelings.

In the next chapter, I will deal more closely with the 'law of attraction.' The law of attraction lends itself excellently to providing practice in energy control. There is already a great deal of literature available on this subject, but I should like to take this opportunity to introduce it to those readers who have not come into contact with this important topic.

> Energy pervades everyone and everything.
> Even our thoughts consist of energy.
> Practice controlling your energy via thoughts and feelings.
> It is very easy!

A SHORT INTRODUCTION

Before dealing with the 'law of attraction,' I should like to summarize the most important steps in the process of synchronization and healing. This will enable you to return to this passage to obtain orientation and obviates the need of constant page turning.

Daily practice

Synchronize yourself daily.

Practice the perception of consciousness (a mental void) a little longer every day.

Before the session

Prepare yourself to do nothing.

Forget your future and past.
Be present in the here and now.

You will be able to transfer your oscillations to the patient.

During the session

Allow the patient to describe the problem exactly.

Formulate your aims mentally. Be <u>precise</u> and <u>positive</u>.

Start the session as you think right. There are no rules or regulations. Be comfortable!

Think the aim a few times during the session. Remain calm.

Decide when the session is finished based upon your instinct.

<u>After the session</u>

Grant your patient enough time to 'come round.'

Quantum energy is still effective days after the treatment.

THE LAW OF ATTRACTION

The media has been discussing something called the 'law of attraction' for a considerable time now. One claim which led me to investigate the matter further posited that

> "Just as with gravity, the law of attraction always operates, whether or not we believe in it. A law of nature cannot be evaded. The same applies to the law of attraction.

You may not accept it, but that does not strip it of its validity."

As I had already experienced things which I would never have held as being possible, I decided to try it out. Is there anything to the law of attraction? Is it possible that our experiences can become part of our lives? Insights from quantum physics would seem to indicate that this is plausible. I should like to outline the basics about the law of attraction.

Similarities attract

Optimistic people attract optimistic people into their lives. Pessimistic people on the other hand, attract people with a negative attitude. This is one of the best examples for this point. Take a look at your circle of friends. Analyse your environment and see what sort of people have gathered themselves around you. You will notice that sourpusses and the gloomy are mostly surrounded by like-minded contemporaries. In the same manner, success attracts success. Happy, open and positive thinking people are much more successful than pessimists. Why so?

Attention is navigation

The things on which you concentrate determine the path taken by your life. If aspire to wealth and plenty, then your subconscious will choose the path necessary to achieve this end. If on the other hand, you concentrate on the problems, lack of money or resentment at your situation, you will harvest exactly these things. Your subconscious always seeks to achieve the object of your attention.

You are responsible for everything in your life

Let me put it another way: you are responsible for your own situation. Misfortune is the result of your having concentrated on the wrong things and having asked the wrong questions. If you find yourself constantly asking "why doesn't the law of attraction work in my case?" then you are concentrating on the aspect of the law not working; in essence, what you do not want. You would be better advised to reformulate the question "what should I do so that this law actually works?" Another example, "why do I work so hard without success?" The focus rests on "much work" and "no success." Ergo you receive exactly the subject of your focus. Ask instead "how can I work less and have greater success?"

Many of these dialogues take part subconsciously. It is thus very important that you analyse your own thoughts and begin to formulate them positively. Ask after what you want, not what you don't want.

HOW CAN I APPLY THIS INSIGHT?

This is an important question. Having become convinced of the existence of this law, we can soon find our own ways to apply it. In order to do this, you need to find out about the law of attraction. Here are a few tips to do so.

Accept responsibility - you are the cause of everything that happens

Most people think that outside factors are responsible for their bad life. They think of themselves as a helpless victim of circumstance. In doing so, they accept this role and attract even more trouble. They concentrate entirely on everything negative. Break this vicious circle: accept responsibility for everything happening around you. This is a difficult thing to do, but it works. Resolve to be happy and allow yourself pleasure every day. The rest is automatic.

Observe your feelings

Observe your 'gut feeling.' If your life takes a direction which feels bad, then it usually is so. Negative feelings are good indicators for things which you do not want. Take exact notice of this. Ensure that you experience good feelings every day. Create optimism. In this way, energy can flow, blockages are released and you achieve what you want.

Invest mental energy

Formulate your aims in writing or a picture. Give them a form that your subconscious can process. It is also helpful to view pictures of things which you would like to have in your life. Visualize and dream - dreams often come true. Why not also for you?

Collect proof of your successes

Keep a sort of diary in which you record everything that you have achieved. Every wish which has come true, even the smallest. Re-read your diary to remind yourself of your successes. You will soon see that the law of attraction actually works. In doing so, you are re-programming your subconscious to focus on success.

Remind yourself of the law on a daily basis

Create a desktop picture or write yourself a note reminding yourself of the law of attraction. In this way, you will learn to start the day with positive thoughts. The more successes you gather in your diary, the more positive your day will begin. You will achieve your goals with ease.

"Pretend that..."

Pretend that you have achieved all your goals. This does not mean that you should spend all your money without thought, should your wish be that to be rich. That would be both fatal and stupid. Simply imagine how you would feel if you were rich. In activating the corresponding feeling, your subconscious will look (and find) ways in which to achieve this. The generation of such conceptions is designed to be fulfilled. Feelings are extremely strong energy!

Do not take the matter too seriously

Just as with healing with quantum energy, you should take care not to take the law of attraction too seriously. Do not work doggedly on success, and do not expect too great a miracle. Think of the whole thing as a game and every-thing will come automatically. Play a game with the universe. You cannot loose anything in this game, but you can win a great deal. Good luck!

Should you wish to find out more about the topic of the 'law of attraction,' there is a lot of material in all good bookshops.

IS IT POSSIBLE TO SUPPORT HEALING IN THIS WAY?

You are probably asking yourself, what the law of attraction has to do with healing through quantum energy. Both take effect in exactly the same fashion via the smallest particles in the universe all which are connected with each other in the strangest of ways. If you use the law of attraction to your advantage and practice daily, and in doing so, fulfil your wishes, you will experience a considerable expansion in your energy potential. The conviction that you are able to achieve things which you had previously held to be impossible will bring considerable successes in healing with quantum energy. Your subconscious will no longer be in any doubt that healing with quantum energy is possible. Every self-experience is doubly effective effect on your patients.

A factor crucial to the success of your work is self-acceptance. No one in the Western world is entirely satisfied with themselves. Some dislike individual aspects of their character; others suffer from a complete inferiority complex.

This dissatisfaction, the lack of self-acceptance costs an extremely large amount of energy, even if we fail to realize it.

Everybody craves recognition and affection. Many confuse these two very different terms. Recognition is given for a good or exceptional achievement. Real affection is given by parents, friends and close ones <u>without</u> the person having done anything to earn it. We often seek to do something spectacular for which we hope to receive affection. That affection is given for what we are, and not what we do often goes unrealized.

Many people feign an entirely different personality because there are things about them which they do not like. They have the impression that others despise them for these characteristics and as a result, they cannot accept themselves. This blockage of the true self, our true personality, robs us of power which could be better used elsewhere. Ask yourself honestly whether there are things which you truly dislike about yourself. Be honest - do you try to achieve affection through achievement? Are there things which you do to please other people? Is it entirely necessary that you do these things?

If you reject the characteristics of your own personality then you open conflict with them, and are forced to expend a considerable amount of energy to avoid or even suppress these things. As soon as you accept yourself as you are, you will be able to release a considerable potential. You are also now in the position to release this potential in other people - through the application of quantum energy.

I should now like to describe a method of self-acceptance.

Sit or lie down in a peaceful location and bring yourself in a light but pleasant trance. You can use the introductory phase of one of the earlier exercises. As soon as you have the feeling that you are relaxed, picture the following sentence.

Thank you – I am as I am

Play with the conception, visualize the letters as becoming smaller or larger, change their colour or let them move. Now repeat this sentence over and over again whilst playing with the picture in front of your inner eye. You can do this out loud or in thoughts. Continue for ten minutes, even if you feel somewhat silly in the process. Now leave your relaxed state and get on with your day, without thinking about this exercise any further. After having performed this exercise once a day for a few days, the words will etch themselves on your subconscious. You will notice how you begin to recite this sentence automatically. Your subconscious has begun to accept itself as it is. Blockages will be released and energy set free. So simple? Yes - it is as simple as that. You need just to try it.

CONCLUSION

What ever you think about the pages that you have just read, whatever you think of esoteric or alternative methods; even if you reject them out of hand. I ask just one thing:

Give it a try!

Even if what I have outlined has the appearance of sheer lunacy and you are unable to find any logical explanation for the effectiveness of such a method:

Give it a chance!

Allow yourself two weeks to experiment with the things that I have just presented to you. You have nothing to lose. No one will see that you have experimented with quantum energy and the law of attraction. How can it hurt?

I hope that in writing this book, I have achieved my goal. My aim was to convince people that we all possess fantastic abilities. These require absolutely no 'initiation' - everyone can take advantage of them. We have probably been carrying these abilities in us for thousands of years. Perhaps there are even higher circles aware of these powers, but who seek to exclude the rest of mankind from benefitting from them. Anything is possible when money and power enter the equation. This is however pure speculation.

One thing is clear:
Everyone has the power to heal!
Including you!

Important note:

Please observe that only those with a specific licence are permitted to treat illnesses. You can play your part by activating our innate powers of self-healing. Do not make any promises! Never advise anybody to stop taking medicines prescribed by a doctor. All illnesses require a medical diagnosis. Do not attempt to prevent anybody from consulting a doctor, alternative practitioner or psychotherapist!

About the author

Ryu Takshashi was born in a small Japanese province in 1962 moved to Germany with his parents at the age of three. Having adapted to a Western lifestyle, he lost all contact to Asian spirituality. After completing his university studies, his life was suddenly by an experience both tragically and happy at the same time. He now helps hundreds of people to activate their powers of self-healing using quantum energy.

<u>For your notice:</u>

For your notice:

<u>For your notice:</u>

CPSIA information can be obtained
at www.ICGtesting.com
Printed in the USA
FSOW04n1319091116
27185FS

9 783839 143636